TRAJECTORY

"HOW TO USE WEBINARS TO SELL AND CLOSE HIGH TICKET OFFERS WITHOUT BEING SALESY"

Practical Guide To Creating An Awesome Webinar That You Can Use Today To Accelerate Your Business Profits.

ROLLAND PETER

Copyright 2018 by Rolland Peter

1st edition

All right reserved. No part of this book may be reproduced or transmitted in any form or by any means without written permission from the author.

Printed in the United States

Limits of liability / disclaimer: The author and publisher of this book have used their best efforts in preparing this material. The author and publisher make no representation or warranties with respect to the accuracy, applicability, or completeness of the contents. They disclaim any warranties (expressed or implied) merchantability for any particular purpose. The author and publisher shall in no event be held liable for any loss or damages including and not limited to special, incidental, consequential, or other damages. This information is compiled from sources believed to be accurate, however the publisher assume no responsibility for error or omissions. The information in this publication is not intended to substitute professional advice. The author and publisher specifically disclaim any liability, loss or risk that is incurred as a consequence, directly or indirectly, of the use and application of any of the content in this book.

FOREWORD by JOY OGEH-HUTFIELD

A 'MAGIC BOOK' for using webinars to sell high ticket offers.
— Joy Ogeh-Hutfield

Most of you have heard the saying 'knowledge is power'. Permit me to ask you to pause and reflect on this statement again. While you ponder, I want you to ask yourselves the following questions:

If knowledge is power, why aren't the most intelligent people in the world the richest or wealthiest?

How many of you would honestly say that what you have studied at school, college or university is what has propelled you to greater heights?

The reality is, having all the knowledge in the world is not enough for you to create the wealth and financial freedom that you want. In the same sense, having all the knowledge available will not necessarily help you transform or make a significant contribution to the world or change lives. It's one thing to know something, it's another thing to do something about what you know — It's called 'TAKING ACTION'. So, perhaps knowledge after all isn't power. KNOWLEDGE APPLIED is power. It is the application of what you know that alternately changes your outlook, your business, your finances and your relationships.

Putting to work what you know gives you the edge and advantage.

As a coach, author, speaker, business woman, wife and mother to three wonderful children acquiring and applying knowledge in the various roles that I play is of the uttermost importance. Knowing how to serve my clients in the highest possible way that will cause them to raise their game comes with stepping out of my comfort zone and applying with wisdom what I have learnt.

Trajectory by Rolland Peter moves you from knowledge and information and compels you with confidence to step out of your comfort zone to dare to see the possibilities by taking MASSIVE ACTION.

In his book TRAJECTORY, Rolland masterfully and expertly gives a step by step strategy using value, desire and trust building questions to help you sell high ticket services using webinar. What has inspired me the most is how Rolland has taken a scary, nerve wrecking and often difficult and complicated subject matter and made it a simple process that anyone, regardless of which expert area they are in can use and apply to get the desired results they are after. Even if you are new to your industry, this book can help you start from zero to selling high ticket services by the time you finish applying the step by step structure to your webinars.

I particularly appreciated the way in which Rolland approached the subject matter of pitching and what he called 'soft sell to empower your audience'. This is an area I believe many people have struggled with over the years, and because of this fear of selling have underplayed their value and not capitalized on great opportunities to serve their customers at the highest level. Trajectory offers a unique way of combating this fear by showing you how to make a persuasive/empowering pitch that focused on developing relationships using primary questions and value building questions instead of aggressively pitching what you want to offer.

If you think you know all about selling high ticket services using webinar, TRAJECTORY will show you how to apply what you know to accelerate you and your business to profitable heights.

My advice:

Read with an open mind

Be expectant and excited

Be prepared to act on the information given

Remember, knowledge is not power. KNOWLEDGE APPLIED IS POWER!

Enjoy the book as much as I have enjoyed the transformation process.

Joy Ogeh-Hutfield

Transformation Coach – Author -Speaker

CEO JOY TRANSFORMATION

www.joytransformationcoach.com

DEDICATION

To my wife Precious, and amazing kids, Caleb, Sharon and Jeremy who have in so many ways inspired and encourage me to keep striving for mastery. You guys means a lot to me than words could express.

And to my many inspiring mentors who have imparted me, with the investment of their personality, knowledge, skills and gifting without measure.

PREFACE

When I got started in business ten years ago in the United Kingdom, the bulk of my time was spent on a daily basis working behind the scenes, until a good friend who knew about the success that I was having at the time, invited me to speak at an event that was being held at the Double Three Hotel by Sheraton in London on e-commerce opportunities- an offer that I gladly accepted. After the conference a lot of people came for inquiries if I have any sort of program that they can buy to learn more about the subject matter. It was then that I remember my first mentor, who posted a comment in a Facebook group that I was a member on what to do when you don't have an online course but want to sell high ticket coaching. He said and I quote "You have to make yourself the product that you intend to sell" So, I offered people an opportunity to join my one-on-one coaching. That conference did set the stage for what I am about to reveal to you in this book.

Some months later, I hosted a live webinar using gotowebinar platform with about 350 registrants, 180 people attended the webinar and twenty one people took the coaching offer at the end of the webinar for $997. The process was simple as I only have a landing page with the offer, including what they will get from joining my e-commerce coaching and a call to action (order now) button. It was a mix of do it yourself (DIY) offers and done with you offers, where I hold live coaching on Skype-then they are requested to implement on what they learnt and done for you offers like building a complete

Shopify store, products upload, configure shipping, pixel installation etc., which I will pass on to my team to carry out. This was just the starting point as I repeated this process many times over with great success. Every sales process is all about testing, Rinse and repeat until you have a sales process machine.

In 2015, I bought a house and soon realise that for us to move into the house, a few essential renovations and a complete remodelling needed to be carried out, which did not come cheap. When we finally moved into the house, I was financially drained because of the huge cost of carrying out the work which was eventually finished after a month. However, we overstayed in the rented house, which means paying an extra month rent and at the same time pay the mortgage for the new house which was undergoing renovation and remodelling. Eventually, we moved into the house not without pressure because the house bills, mortgage including my business bills are failing due simultaneously. The funds were not available in the bank for my direct debit to go through. This was when I decided to experiment with high ticket offers using webinars.

I reached out to a joint venture partner who mailed his list to attend the webinar which was scheduled. I can remember telling my wife that this webinar was going to be life changing and destiny altering. The format of this webinar was different from the previous ones which were basically sales webinars, in the sense that instead of selling on the webinar, an offer is made for them to apply to work with me directly. So anyone who requires help to implement what I taught on the webinar is required to complete an application, then a phone appointment will be scheduled for us to have free discovery session to determine if we are a good fit to work together. We received eight applications, then closed three potential students at $5,000 each and they made the payment through PayPal a few hours later on after receiving the invoice.

This was how I bounced back to business from a very close shaved with bankruptcy and was able to sustain a growth "Trajectory" in my business using the strategies which are outlined in this book. I hold an MBA in International business from a leading UK university, and did not need to go out and seek a job with my qualifications. Using webinars to sell high ticket offers made my MBA redundant.

The strategies outlined in this book are not theory, it took over five years to perfect after hosting a lot of webinars which are my primary tools for high ticket customer acquisition strategy. Also, these strategies got refined through continuous learning and going through a lot of training on webinars from the best and most prolific experts in the webinar space.

What makes this book different is the way that I have broken the steps down into actionable steps in a way that you will be able to apply the strategy regardless of your niche or service offerings- whether you are a coach, consultant or providing professional services.

More often than not, you can use webinar to sell just about anything and the most popular is to sell online courses, SaaS (Software as a service), physical products etc. with specific methodology which is very predictable because the sales close are usually stalks of what the potential customer will get with the value in terms of the dollar amount, leading up to when the real price of the offer is revealed, then followed by a call to action for them to buy. This webinar sales model is effective to sell products priced anywhere from $100-$1,000, but if you have an offer that's priced higher than the aforementioned numbers then, this book is for you.

However, this webinar model is what I have always used to attract prospect into my multifaceted coaching which has helped majority of my clients scale their businesses to new levels of success which is ultimately the real transformational impact. It's not all about delivery an awesome webinar to attract your ideal prospects but most importantly to get the client results. That is what this book is all about, "it's a strategy."

Strategy is about first analysing and then experimenting, trying, learning, and experimenting some more.

-Ian C. McMillan and Rita Gunther McGrath

Contents

Structure of your high-ticket webinar xix

Overview xxi

CHAPTER ONE: Core Structure One – Introduction 1
    Give your webinar a title 1
    Tell the audience your credentials 2
    Make a primary promise 2

CHAPTER TWO: Core Structure Two - Setup 3
    Why should your audience stick around? 3
    Reveal your bonus 4

CHAPTER THREE: Core Structure Three - Opportunity switch outcome and concerns 5
    Restate the outcome your audience can expect you to deliver 5
    Add a caveat 6
    Put any outcome-related concerns to bed 6

CHAPTER FOUR: Core Structure Four – Seed-sowing and Pre-framing 9
    Let your webinar audience know you're here to help 9
    Pre-frame your ideal prospect 10
    Address the issue of self-doubt 11

CHAPTER 5: Core Structure Five - Story telling 13
Tell them about your journey 13
The power of the underdog 14

CHAPTER SIX: Core Structure Six - Content 15
Pre-frame your offer 15
Drill down 15
Use third-party data to validate your point 16
Compress your content into 3 or more secrets 17
How to craft your 3 secrets 18

CHAPTER SEVEN: Core Structure Seven: Pre-Pitch 21
Ask them the primary question 21
Define their aspirations 22
Introduce a bonus 23
Start crafting your closes 24

CHAPTER EIGHT: Core Structure Eight - The Pitch 25
Soft sell to empower your audience 25
Deliver the pitch, and don't forget the bonus 25
Outline how things go from here 27
Reinforce your value 28

CHAPTER NINE: Core Strategy Nine – The Close 29
Persuade them you're on their side 29

    Anchor the value of your offer 32

    Link to your application page 33

    Tell them what they really need to know..33

    Always remember the importance of outcomes.......................................34

    Extended offer and bonuses 34

What comes next..39

    Eliciting information 39

    Open-ended questions 40

    Qualifying questions 41

    Questions to establish rapport, trust and credibility 41

Conclusion 43

RESOURCES...45

References 47

HOW TO USE WEBINARS TO SELL AND CLOSE HIGH TICKET OFFERS WITHOUT BEING SALESY

In this book, you are going to discover how to create webinars to sell high ticket services and at the same time deliver valuable content to help people by using an application system. This is quite a combination and if you use this method, you won't go wrong. Webinars are quickly becoming one of the most powerful tools in the professional marketer's arsenal. Regardless of your industry or niche, webinars are proving to be an incredibly effective way to build your brand's exposure and authority, while generating sales and revenue.

Throughout this book, I'm going to assume that you'll be doing your webinars live initially, before moving on to evergreen or automated webinars. The main reason, you might consider hosting live webinars is that, you can have a live questions and answers (Q&A) sessions to resolve objections and doubts. This will definitely provide the most value for your customers. At this initial stage, you'll be able to help more people and, if you do live webinars properly, you are likely to get the majority of your applications for your services during the live Q&A sessions at the end.

I want to assume that your webinar audience is a cold audience, meaning they don't know you prior to attending your webinar. And the most interesting thing about webinars is that, they can move an audience from cold to warm, then hot instantly, which is why I recommend using them for your customer acquisition strategy. And your warm traffic sources are usually from either your email list or joint venture partners, which will definitely get you more conversions using webinars.

First of all, what you're going to need in order to host your webinar is a webinar hosting platform, like gotowebinar.com, zoom.us or webinarjam to name but a few. Using any of these platforms is very straightforward and they have a lot of video tutorials to help you get started. Secondly, you'll require a whiteboard, which I'll call the new pen and paper, or a traditional notepad and pen to write your ideas down. Better still you can use a mind mapping software which is my preferred option.

The very next thing you're going to need is a clear understanding of the transformational results and outcome that your ideal client need to achieve. Using the webinar delivery model of selling high ticket offers, you'll have to figure out the fastest, most efficient route possible to move them from point A to point B and there are certain deliverables involved in that process. At the planning stages when putting your offers together for the webinar, you should have already figured out these deliverables.

The final thing you're going to need is PowerPoint in PC or Keynote in Mac because webinars are delivered in slideshow format. Do ensure to record your live webinars within the webinar platforms as the replay will come handy to retarget people who registered but did not show up or left the webinar before the pitch and at any given stage of your webinar funnel.

Structure of your high-ticket webinar

Let's get started.

First thing we're going to do is talk about the structure of your webinar. Now, these kinds of webinars are different from traditional sales webinars, but the differences between them are not too far away from each other. The major differentiating factor is that high ticket webinars are based on outcome or transformation as the case maybe. So, we're going to use a structured approach of nine (9) steps which you will learn about in this book.

Here is the overview of the Nine Core Structures of your High Ticket Webinar Presentation.

Overview

Core structure one – Introduction

Core structure two – Setup

Core structure three – Opportunity switch outcome and concerns

Core structure four – Seed-sowing and pre-framing

Core structure five – Story telling

Core structure six – Content

Core structure seven – Pre-pitch

Core structure eight – Pitch

Core structure nine – Close

Now let me walk you through the nine steps in more detail.

CHAPTER ONE

Core Structure One – Introduction

Give your webinar a title

The first logical thing to do is to give your webinar the right title. It is advisable to make your webinar title an opportunity switch and it should always be outcome-based: Look at these examples:

'How You Can Profit From One Evergreen Business Opportunity of the Decade!

"How to" OR "How" then immediately fill in the benefit.

Also, 'How to————without——————-' is always a good formula to create your opportunity switch outcome-based headline for a webinar presentation.

The how-to headline should appeals to the inherent need or problem that your ideal client wants to solve. The key is to focus on a pain point and primary promise to fulfil that need or want. However, be aware that the how-to must highlight the benefit or final result, not the process itself. Do refer to a copyrighting book to learn how to write great headlines that converts.

Tell the audience your credentials

At this stage, after the introduction of your title, immediately tell your audience your credentials: your names and areas of specialisation. Keep it simple. Here's an example:

Welcome to today's webinar !The title of my webinar is' How To Lose Weight Without Exercising in No Time At All Or Giving Up Your Favourite Carbs 'and that's exactly what I will be revealing in this webinar .Now ,for those who don't know me ,my name is Rolland and I work specifically with women who are over ,40 to help them lose weight and stay fit ,amongst other things.

Make a primary promise

Having made your introduction, you will immediately transition to make a primary promise. This does not have to be exaggerated, like 'How to make a seven-figure income within 24 hours if you deploy my strategy'. This is not the kind of promise I'm talking about. The type of promise I'm suggesting you use goes like this:

You must have come on this webinar today due to the fact that you've not properly profiled your ideal client to the extent that you are now attracting them into your business. But the reality of the situation is you can actually attract high-paying clients on demand consistently into your business, twelve months of the year, on autopilot, using the very simple marketing strategies that I will be revealing.

This is a perfect example of how to make a primary promise that will resonate with your audience. The one I've shown you above is for the purposes of illustration only as you'll have to come up with something relevant to your own offer.

CHAPTER TWO

Core Structure Two - Setup

Why should your audience stick around?

At this stage, you have to let your audience know about the subject matter you're going to be talking about on the webinar. The main reason you'll want to do this is to sustain their interest to get their full attention. What you're really doing here is setting up a strong case for them being here and what the expectations of your webinar are.

An effective way to achieve this is to say:

Here's what we're going to talk about on this webinar. Specifically, I'm going to reveal to you three core strategies to present your offer in a 'non-salesy' way. We're also going to talk about how to implement these three core strategies to get the desired outcome, and about the mindset of a high ticket service provider.

Obviously, this is just an example you can model – you don't have to follow the exact format as you will always implement what works best for the client you plan to serve at the highest level. The ultimate goal is to make sure your prospects know the immediate benefits of staying with the webinar right to the end.

Reveal your bonus

Another strategy that you should consider using in this section is to reveal your bonus, which could be a template, cheatsheet or Pdf that will complement your offer at the end of the webinar. After you have told them what you are going to be teaching, you can position the bonus you're going to be giving away along these lines:

At the end of this presentation, I will be giving away my free cheatsheet on how you can serve the client at the highest level without being stuck on endless live calls, so that you can implement the strategies you'll discover from this webinar. So stay with me till the end!

Most importantly, your free give-away must be congruent with your core offer.

CHAPTER THREE

Core Structure Three - Opportunity switch outcome and concerns

Restate the outcome your audience can expect you to deliver

In this section we are going to craft the opportunity switch outcome and concerns. The first thing you want to do is to state the outcome again:

You can definitely sell high ticket coaching but you have to be knowledgeable about what you're doing to do it right.

I strongly recommend that you start with this opening statement. The premise behind this recommendation is that it will establish your authority as an expert and demonstrate to your audience that this webinar is not just hype. Here is the reason why? when they first come across your ads or emails about the webinar, they're going to have concerns. Your legitimacy will be under scrutiny, coupled with their inner fears and doubts about whether they can really do this. You want to let them know, straight up, that in fact, *not* everybody can do this. Because what you're going to let them know then is that, *you* will teach them the things they have to do, in other to execute the strategy successfully.

Add a caveat

The way to do this is to position the statement of the desired outcome with a caveat: 'Yes, you can write your book in one week, but you have to know how you can achieve this particular outcome'. That's the caveat, then we want to address their actual concerns. You do that by saying, 'now, let's talk about writing your book in one week.'

There are going to be a lot of questions and objections about how they can accomplish this task of book writing. You have to be very skilled to write a book in one week or, better still, you have to hire a ghost writer to write it for you and even then, it's going to take several months to accomplish.

So your logical response to these pertinent questions will be:

Well, that's incorrect, because I'm living proof that you can write your book in one week. As a matter of fact, I got a friend to interview me for an hour and I transcribed the audio to text, then got it proofread and copy edited. That was how I wrote my book. However, I don't consider myself an expert writer and you don't have to be either.

Put any outcome-related concerns to bed

Obviously, this is just an example. You have to restate your outcome with the caveat and then start addressing the concerns your prospect may have. The reason we allay those concerns is that we know they are going to have a lot of objections. So, figure out what objections are prevalent in your industry and raise them before your prospects do. Address them directly in this section of your webinar.

Don't overthink the process, and here's another example that you can model:

I know that some of you might have some concerns like: How can I be a great seminar presenter when I'm not a native English speaker and my spoken English is not fluent enough? Well, later on in the webinar I'm going to teach you exactly how to achieve your goals even though you might have that kind of challenge. So don't go anywhere!

Make sure you address this concern as promised or you stand the risk of losing the credibility you built up initially.

CHAPTER FOUR

Core Structure Four – Seed-sowing and Pre-framing

Let your webinar audience know you're here to help

This section of the core strategy webinar structure should not take more than five to ten minutes.

Seed-sowing is where you mention the fact that you're going to offer to help your prospects. There are two reasons you want to do this. First, you want them to start thinking along these lines: 'Okay, maybe I can work with this person because s/he's offering a shoulder to lean on.' It makes sense to let them know upfront that you will be selling something so that it doesn't come as surprise to them. This strategy could equally work as a filter because you're going to lose some people on the webinar at this point, that is, some people will drop off. But guess what? Your ideal prospect will stay till the end.

Here's how you do it. Suppose you're a coach, helping specific service providers. This is what you might say:

I want you to know that when we're done, I'm going to specially invite you to consider the opportunity of working together on your programme and price point, so that you can get that ideal client, who will pay you what are you worth.

Pre-frame your ideal prospect

Now, immediately, you have to use the seed sowing: telling them what they have to do and say in order to succeed. Here's how you can structure your sentence:

Listen, I want you to understand right now, I can't work with everybody and this isn't a big disguised sales pitch. As a matter of fact, the truth of the matter is that in order for you to become a premium agency operator, whether you and I work together or not, you have to have these three things.

Now you're going to talk about those three things. Here's an example which is relevant to my own business. I'd say:

Now, listen. In order to actually have a successful business, where you sell high ticket offers to your client, whether you and I decide to work together or not or you decide to figure it out by yourself, it doesn't matter. Either way, you've got to have these three things in place.

First of all, you have to be able to actually help your clients get results, because results are paramount to selling high ticket offers. It's not possible to build a business around nothing these days.

Secondly, you must have a budget to run ads on Facebook and be ready to learn how to split test ads to find a winner. Whether you and I work together or not, or you decide to do this on your own, there're going to be times on your journey where you're going to experience failures.

Also, you have to be prepared to host webinars even if you've never done a webinar before. You might actually have to talk to people one-on-one about your services.

You might doubt your abilities from time to time which is peculiar to most people. The fact of the matter is, everybody is going to face some form of challenges. If you're not willing to push through these challenges or leave your own comfort zone, success will be far-fetched. It doesn't matter if you are a student of mine. This is just to be upfront with you guys.

Also, listen, you will need to make a commitment to yourself not to let your self-doubt stop you from having what you really want.

Address the issue of self-doubt

Another point to consider passing across to your prospects which is a must in this section, no matter what you're selling is this – whether you're helping a dental practice or chiropractor to get leads, helping people lose weight etc. When we're helping people get from point A to point B, oftentimes their self-doubt is among the limiting beliefs that will stop them in their tracks. It's really important to address this and make it part of the pre-framing.

Now, you will observe that in the seed-sowing and pre-framing model above, there was no mention of money. Neither did we talk about 'applying' or make any mention of scarcity, like 'limited space'. All we're doing is:

1) seeding the fact that you're going to be willing to help them personally

2) Start to pre-frame the fact that, to be a good fit for your service, they have to meet certain criteria's and, most importantly, it's not for everybody. Now we've established that, we can wrap the rest of our presentation around it. This is the huge pre-frame – **is more like saying ,-** You've to qualify yourself to me. It's a choice you have to make. You can work with me or go ahead to keep trying to make it work on your own, but here's what you've got to do either way'. For now, leave it as an open loop.

CHAPTER Five

Core Structure Five - Story telling

Tell them about your journey

To proceed, this is the part where you tell your back story which is called the hero's journey. Now you want to let them how you got to this point in your career. If you have a story of loss and redemption, that's perfect. Ask for permission to tell your back story by saying', would it be okay if I tell you a little bit about myself'? Then summarise your back story of struggles and success and what you have achieved, based on what your audience wants to achieve, but keep it short so that you don't bore them. Remember: this is not about you. However, a student of mine has success with a very long hero's journey story of about 45 minutes long but you have to test to find out what will work best for the audience you plan to serve at the highest level.

In Russell Brunson's book, *The Expert's Secrets*, he talked about the hero's journey, which has three important phases: character (backstory), conflict (journey to achievement) and desire (transformation). (Do you remember that at the beginning of the webinar we talked about the transformation?) So if you can craft a good story of loss and redemption featuring yourself or someone you've worked with around your topic, this is definitely where you want to tell it.

Everybody has a backstory to tell. Personally, I usually tell the story of how I lost large sums of money to a dodgy supplier in Hong Kong when I started my eCommerce business, which affected my circumstances to the extent that I almost dropped out of my MBA programme, but made an incredible comeback. Then, subsequently, when I thought I had it all figured out, my Amazon seller account was shut down, my business stalled, I went broke and found myself back at square one until I met my mentor, and the rest is history.

The story of loss and redemption is probably one of the most powerful storylines in the history of storytelling – an incredible story of how the underdog finally made it.

The power of the underdog

Chances are that if you're reading this book right now, you're an underdog. So you want your audience to be able to relate to you. The main purpose of this section is to present yourself as relatable by putting yourself in their shoes: if you can make it, so can they. Life's events were not always in your favour but you've graduated from the School of Hard Knocks and they should be listening to you because you've been through it. You're actually a practitioner. This is what you're trying to achieve with your story.

Feel free to tell a great story and the epiphany you experienced or the new opportunities you discovered in the process. However, don't just make up a story if you don't have any real ones to share; just leave this part of the webinar out or share a story of a client's success.

CHAPTER SIX

Core Structure Six - Content

Pre-frame your offer

After you have told your story, progress to delivering your content. You've already started setting this up, but now we need to wrap this content around the facts that:

1. They have the capacity to do it.

2. They can't do it if they are not confident enough to get it right.

3. You're going to help them make it happen, if they're lucky enough to be a good fit for your services.

4. You can't work with everybody and they're going to have to be a good fit, by meeting some essential criteria.

Drill down

You want to begin this section by really working a problem. Here's an example of doing this.

Okay, so now let's really get into it. Let's talk about the seven ways to grow a successful eCommerce business. A lot of people right now are struggling, and inundated with cart abandonments which they are unable to recover, in spite of the fact that they are using the best cart abandonment apps. They have done the audience research and product research to enable them to match product to market, meaning they have good products that people want to buy. But they're not making sales. Or they are driving a lot of traffic to their online store and the traffic is not converting.

Whatever it is, if this is your particular experience, be aware that you're not alone. Chances are that it's not your fault, and we can fix this problem but you've to do it right. This is more like a standard formulation to handle objections and the technique goes like this:

1. Tell them" I understand how you… ."**leef**

2. Tell them about someone else who **tlef** the same way initially.

3. Then tell them how that person **dnuof** that when they did what you wanted/bought the product ,they got what they wanted.

Use third-party data to validate your point

Now that you've identified and clarified the problem, it makes perfect sense to verify that the problem really exists by using third-party data to authenticate your point. We're still going to use the eCommerce business analogy. Here's an example.

E-commerce offers fantastic revenue opportunities due to the fact that it is a business at scale, the ability to be open 24/7 and traditionally fewer overheads as compared to bricks-and-mortar retailing. Yet, despite the fact that more than 12 million Australian consumers shop online – and we are experiencing year-over-year double digit growth in online shopping – according to *Entrepreneur* magazine, a huge number of eCommerce businesses are struggling to be profitable, or in many cases, survive. So, clearly, we have a problem here.

That's an example of using third-party data to authenticate or validate the problem. Essentially, after you have tied your content to this pre-frame. Then progress by saying it's important for you to pay close attention to learn how you can fix this problem'. You need to really point out that hey, this problem is serious. So now, once they're in that frame of mind, they're really willing to listen to you teach them exactly how to solve it.

Compress your content into 3 or more secrets

Remember that your content is always outcome-based and, as a rule, you have to deliver it using a transition. Essentially, since we have limited time on this webinar, I have to compress my ideas into three secrets which you will learn and be able to implement for an immediate outcome.

As an illustration, your content could be 'Three Secrets To Scaling Your eCommerce Business To Seven Figures, Without Working 24/7, Thereby Securing a Better Work-Life Balance'.

Here is how you come up with the three secrets that you will build your content around: find the three core limiting beliefs or pain points relative to the particular service you are going to be offering.

Pain Point 1

eCommerce business is labour-intensive and difficult to run.

Turn this pain into a 'how to solve the pain point': this is how you come up with your secret.

Secret #1

How to hire skilled workers to run your eCommerce business for under $5 an hour, so that you don't have to work 24/7 and still achieve your work-life balance.

Pain Point 2

It's difficult to get people to order several products in one go.

Secret #2

How to increase the average order value without increasing your existing ads spend using a funnel system to sell your product.

Paint Point 3

You need to buy and hold inventory to run a successful eCommerce business.

Secret #3

How to source and sell eCommerce products in any niche without holding inventory.

How to craft your 3 secrets

Make a list of the limiting beliefs or pain points that the niche you are serving is experiencing, then provide the corresponding answer in a 'how-to' format hinged on curiosity as this will make them stay put and listen till the end. Don't get too specific; you don't want to overwhelm them as they haven't yet committed to learn right now. This is just so they can dip their toes in the water. Hence, you want to identify the pain points, create the three secrets for them to get the desired outcome and, by giving enough data, let them actually see themselves achieving the desired result.

So create your three secrets, then teach them what they have to do in order to get through those pain points or limiting beliefs in order to achieve the transformation that they so desperately desire.

To sum up this chapter, provide your audience with accompanying content for each of the three secrets for a good 30-45 minutes across many slides, using a lot of examples and great graphics. Make it entertaining for them. Don't bore them! Make sure they realise that they can do this and that you're available to help them.

CHAPTER SEVEN

Core Structure Seven: Pre-Pitch

Ask them the primary question

This page is a prelude to the pitch, which is why it's titled the pre-pitch-more like you marinade the offer. You won't give a full pitch of your offering here but just a warm-up. As a rule, you will start with a primary question, which is going to be the single biggest question related to their outcome.

Let's use the 'Three Secrets To Scaling Your eCommerce Business To Seven Figures, Without Working 24/7, Thereby Securing a Better Work-Life Balance' as an example. Start like this:

You're probably saying to yourself: great, so I know these three secrets but what do I need to know and do? What's the exact formula for scaling my eCommerce business to seven figures? And how do I secure a better work-life balance?

Depending on the services you are offering or intend to offer, your primary question will obviously be different. The main reason you're asking this primary question is to reiterate the importance of what you're sharing and subsequently sustain your guests' attention.

Define their aspirations

Immediately after leading by asking your primary question, begin to implement in the next slide a list of aspiration-building questions, as shown below:

By now I've told you the three secrets to building, growing and scaling an eCommerce business to seven figures, thereby securing a better work-life balance. But listen, you know, there's a lot more to it. It's not just about learning these three secrets. There are more questions we need to be asking ourselves as well.

Question 1: What will I be known for?

Question 2: How do I create a brand?

Question 3: Who's my ideal customer?

Question 4: What type of products and services will my ideal customer buy?

So if you're coaching digital agency owners how to get more clients that they can sell lead generation, you might make question number one and two 'who do I want to be known as in my industry environment?' and 'do I want to be known for getting clients results?' Others include: 'who's my ideal customer?' 'Which kind of clients do I want to work with?' 'What kind of leads do my customers want?' 'What other services will my client want?' and 'what other offers can be bundled to ascend my customers?'

These are the value, desire and trust-building questions that you want to have your prospects asking themselves. When they ask these questions, they're stepping into that scenario, and they're starting to think along these lines. what are the possibilities for my business? What are the possibilities for my life as it pertains to the subject matter that has been discussed here on today's webinar?'

Introduce a bonus

Having progressed from asking the primary question to asking the aspirational or value-building questions in our pre-pitch session, now we have to progress into the pre-pitch with a bonus. The perfect transition would be to say:

As you are all aware, this information is of vital importance and I want to help you find your own answers to these questions by giving you a free forty five minutes discovery session, where I can provide coaching to structure your offers to attract your ideal client.

Give something of value away as a great bonus. It could be a free web-class, a free course, cheatsheet or Pdf. The idea that your bonuses communicate should strike your prospects as new, unique and different. They should find it startling, arresting and compelling; something they have to stop and say to themselves, 'I must have that!'

Here's an example:

I want to help you find your own answers in regard to selling high ticket offers by giving you my template, entitled 'How to get your customers to dominate your sales calls by asking relevant questions, so that you can close them easily'. It's valued at $3,500, due to the fact, that this is what every customer in my sales funnel is worth to me.

Start crafting your closes

After you've introduced the bonus, you will move from teaching to the sales presentation, which is the pitch. You'll present your offer in a precise format called 'the stack' by crafting some unique closes that are proven to persuade people to take the clear-cut actions necessary to achieve desired outcomes.

CHAPTER EIGHT

Core Structure Eight - The Pitch

Soft sell to empower your audience

The pitch is a progression from the pre-pitch and even at this stage of the presentation, you have to use a soft-sell, which is a subtle, yet persuasive, low-pressure method of selling. It's important to empower your audience: to offer them a way to go further if they're ready to succeed with the solution that you offer. Not everyone will be at a point where they will take advantage of this, but not one member of your webinar audience wants to feel 'stuck', as if there's no way to really run with the information that you've given them in the course of the presentation. The basic premise of soft selling is that your focus is on developing relationships using the primary questions and value-building questions, instead of aggressively pitching your offer.

Deliver the pitch, and don't forget the bonus

Start with a soft pitch on this slide by saying, 'here is how you can work with me'. Provide the URL for them to apply on the slide and while you're showing that slide, here's what you want to say.

Firstly, I want to let you know that this course is not available to buy from me today and I don't want you to feel like you're in the middle of a big sales pitch. The fact of the matter is, before you and I can work together I want to talk to you personally to ensure that we're a good fit. Use the displayed URL on the screen to apply to work with me. Now, here's how it is going to work.

First of all, I have an in-depth masterclass, so you and I aren't going to just work together for a day. We're actually going to work together for six weeks, or for eight weeks, or for however long it's going to be. I'm not going to send you a home study course or anything; you and I are going to be working very closely together over the course of two months. There's a lot involved in that, and it's not for everybody. **evisnepxe etiuq yllaer s'tI**. Like I said, it's not available for purchase because it's a bespoke live virtual masterclass. In order for us to work together, you will need to schedule an appointment for a breakthrough session with me to enable us to determine if we're a good fit.

You can apply to become a client of mine, by using the URL displayed on the screen. Immediately after you apply, here's what's going to happen. You're going to get a phone call from a member of my team who will schedule a time in the immediate future, within the next 24 hours, for us to get together on the phone for about 25 minutes.

During this breakthrough session, some questions will be put across to you and you'll have the opportunity to ask some questions as well. Be aware that, there are about a thousand people on this webinar tonight and I can only work with the first 20 people that will apply now. Whether or not you're one of them, either way it's totally okay with me. But I wanted to let you know that you do have the opportunity to apply to work with me, and when you become a client of mine, you will immediately receive my free cheat sheet on 'How you can serve your clients at the highest level without Being Stuck on Endless Live Calls', which is the bonus I promised to give you at the beginning of this webinar.

Remember, this was the early bonus seed we sowed. All things considered, for the purposes of high ticket selling services using webinars, this is how you will deliver that pitch. While you do so, your slide is up with your link to an application form or use an appointment schedule software like *acuity, scheduleonce or calenderly*.

Outline how things go from here

Also, you want to briefly describe what they will get by mentioning how you'll proceed if you and your prospect decide you're a good fit for each other. Don't go into the full details at this point; just say something along these lines:

We're going to be working together for eight weeks. Every week, I will schedule a live virtual coaching call and you will get the recordings of the training delivered to your members area after 24 hours of the coaching call, to include assignments. You will have access to a private Facebook group where you can ask questions and bounce ideas off each other. Furthermore, I will schedule a bi-weekly virtual question and answer session on Zoom with every member of the class just to provide you with guidance along the way.

And if you think that the strategies and insights you've received so far in this webinar were helpful, wait until you get into the actual masterclass that will run for eight weeks. Then we're going to meet together, in London, for a live workshop with this particular group of students that are going to join this masterclass today for a final session and networking to build a vital network going forward.

(You may not necessarily have a live event as this is for the purposes of illustration.)

What is more, I'm not going to give you a sales pitch about it. Use the link at the bottom of the page to apply now. You will receive a call on Skype,

Phone or any of your preferred option and you can ask any questions you have. You will be asked some questions as well to ensure that we can work together.

Reinforce your value

At this stage, this is where you reinforce your time, pressure and scarcity, and then you move on:

Considering the fact that we have about a thousand people on this webinar, the available spots are going to fill up fast and I can only take a few clients. So if you're interested in this, go ahead and apply. If you're still on the fence, wondering if it's right for you, stay with me as I'm going to reveal to you a few more secrets to help you gain an unfair advantage. So, let's keep moving.

CHAPTER NINE

Core Strategy Nine – The Close

Persuade them you're on their side

On this slide, you will need to apply the 'One sentence persuasion course' by Blair Warren in your close. Here it is:

People will do anything for those who encourage their dreams, confirm their fears, confirm their suspicions, and help them throw rocks at their enemies. They are the tools for anyone who wants to connect with others and most importantly, make the connections to pay off.

The following is my own paraphrased version of Blair Warren's words.

Encourage their dreams

Parents more often than not tell their children, the dream, vision or purpose they should pursue in life should be something sensible. The children normally follow the path their parents have suggested until others show up who encourage their dream: 'You love comedy, this is your passion. Just follow your dream! Why in the world do you want to become an engineer?'

When this happens, who do you think has more power? Parents? Or the others who encourage their dreams?

Justify their failures

Several million usually applaud Dr Phil as he tells people to take responsibility for their mistakes. Meanwhile, millions of people are desperately looking for someone to take the responsibility off their shoulders and tell them it is not their fault. It will be argued that taking responsibility is critical to gaining control of one's own life, but assuring others that they are not responsible is essential for gaining influence over theirs.

Allay their fears

It is almost impossible to give your attention to something else when you are afraid. Most of the time, our natural response is to tell a person not to be afraid and expect that to do the trick.

Does it work? My guess is as good as yours as the problem remains unsolved.

But there are those who realise this and pay special attention to our fears and resolve not to casually tell us that everything will be alright. Instead, they work with us until our fears subside. They present evidence, they offer support, they tell us stories of transformation experienced by people who have been in similar circumstances. They do not tell us how to feel with an expectation that we will indeed feel that way. The question is: when you're afraid, which type of person would you prefer to be with?

Confirm their suspicions

One favourite remark we often make is 'I knew it!' There's usually a surge of 'aha!' when someone confirms what we suspect, we are naturally inclined to be attracted to the person who helped make that sudden realisation come alive.

Help them throw rocks at their enemies

Nothing bonds like having a common enemy. Although it sounds ugly, it's true just the same. Those who understand this can utilise it. Those who don't understand it – or worse, understand but refuse to address it – are throwing away one of the most effective ways of connecting with others. No matter what you may think of the fact, rest assured that people have enemies. All people. It has been said that everyone you meet is engaged in a great struggle. The thing they are struggling with is their enemy. Whether that's another individual, a group, an illness, a setback, a rival philosophy or religion or what have you, if you're engaged in a struggle, you want others to join you. Those who do become more than friends; they become partners. The fact is, while these insights seem like common sense, they are anything but common practice. Except among master persuaders.

Here's an example of the persuasion statement in action.

You must have tried everything that the guru recommends and failed… it's not your fault, but that is not to say you cannot achieve your dreams of running a successful social media agency by modelling what's proven to work. My offer is a Done-With-You programme, which is more like hand holding, looking over my shoulders all the way until you succeed.

What we have done is to throw rocks at the enemy – the gurus – justify their failures and encourage their dreams. You can use one or several of these persuasion tips to craft your webinar close to move the prospect from point A to point B.

Anchor the value of your offer

So, let's go back to anchoring the value of what you have to offer and why your prospects should take you up on it: 'Listen. You always want to take the simplest path from point A to point B.'

Example #1 Keeping it simple

After all, you have two choices to make: follow the simple proven path, which is the option for us to work together; or do it the hard way by chasing every shiny object due to the proliferation of information out there with the hope that you may find what works. Usually, when you try to complicate matters, you never even get started because you are bogged down in the details. Reiterate that the simplest path is often the best.

Example #2 Benefit of commitment to learning with you

In essence, the job at hand is to reveal the importance of learning everything they can about the outcome of the transformation that they want to achieve; committing not only to learn but also to take massive action through implementation. Hence, committing to learning also equals investing in the education to get there. So every one of these closes backs up the soft pitch that you will make.

The next slide is a potential list of benefits that your guests will get from working with you.

Here's an example of what this slide should say:

Let's do this together. Let's help you to create your own blue ocean, your own unique market. Let me help you build your own group of loyal fans, cultivate a tribe of people who are loyal to your business, your branding, your products, your philosophy. Let me help you discover how you can create a lifestyle business that can thrive with a relatively small dedicated team who will help you build your business empire.. Let me show you how to make this year your best year ever as a consultant, coach etc.

The purpose of this slide is to show them the future benefits of working with you and to ask them to let you show them how to achieve those milestones.

Link to your application page

Subsequently, place your link to the application page on every single slide from this point going forward, so they can see it while you're delivering your presentation. Because now we've given a soft pitch, just saying, 'Let me show you how to do this', it's time to start going deep into the official pitch.

Tell them what they really need to know

Let's talk now about the pitch – the official pitch. One great way to lead into it is the phrase: 'Here's what you're going to get from working with me'. And you want to start with a single slide with an overview of what's included when you do this (for example, eight weeks of live coaching personally with me, to include an exclusive two-day live mastermind and networking meeting with me and your fellow students). The next slide will provide more detail, with the specifics of what they are going to be getting. Since we are using an eight-week mastermind example, you want to have eight slides, with each one following the format below.

How to create your own blue oceans, so that you can serve a niche audience that that will place value on the results you can bring them.

Benefit bullet point #1: To enable you to create buyers on demand

Benefit bullet point #2: Command a premium price

Benefit bullet point #3: Build a tribe around your brand

This is just an example. You are not restricted to three benefits; by all means come with as many benefits as possible for each of the slides.

Always remember the importance of outcomes

Remember people want transformation and the last thing you would want to do, is to make false income claims. Don't make any false income claim, to be compliant with regulatory requirements, and don't say anything that might be misconstrued as a false income claim. However, you can add an income disclaimer at the beginning that goes along the lines that your results or your clients' results are typical and that there is no guarantee that they will achieve the same results or income goal.

Extended offer and bonuses

Further more, we are pitching what your prospects will get in the various weeks using benefit bullet points. You should have a slide for the bonuses immediately after the first week's overview slide. Also, you want to pitch the bonuses just as you would sell the application to work with you. It makes sense for every bonus to have its own slide, to include the URL to your application page.

You don't need to go into the detail; just 'here is why I'm giving you this bonus.' Provide the value amount of the bonus; justify the value by saying it's worth x dollars amount because that is the value you or your clients get from using it. Explain how it's going to help them get the transformation; here's why you want it; here's the value of it; here's why you want to get it now, using this link.

Having done a couple of pre-pitches, seeded early on with the bonus and done the main pitch, it's time to add some fast action bonus by giving a price break.

Price Break Close Slide

Earlier on, it was mentioned that the programme is not available for sale, cannot be bought off the shelves and is expensive. We said it's only available through an application, after the client is assessed to determine if they are a good fit. Offering a price break is usually a deal breaker and a clue to what the offer might potentially cost. Let's proceed by saying: 'I want you to realise that I will reward people who take action immediately by filling out my application for an appointment. So the first 5 or 10 people to apply will get a $500 discount,' or whatever. Doing this gets people to apply quickly. Once you've done that, you have a new slide where you add a surprise bonus. You can say something along these lines:

When I was putting this webinar together, I realised how important it is for me to personally support you. I derive a lot of joy when I get success stories from people. So that's why I've decided to really do as much as I possibly could to enlist you in this journey to get what you truly want.

And because I'm committed to your success, I've decided to add a few more surprise bonuses.

Good examples of surprise bonuses are a forty-five minutes of Zoom live calls, Skype access, one-on-one consulting or whatever the case may be. Afterwards, lead your audience into the live question and answer session.

Last Slide of the Webinar

The last slide should have a headline titled Q&A, with a big link to your order page on it, clearly visible, and that's it. During your Q&A, you can see their questions typed in. A little piece of honest advice: don't take irrelevant questions. Don't take questions that could get people off the topic. Only answer questions that are geared towards getting people to apply.

Look for valuable, valid objections that you can clearly help them overcome, make sure you look for objections and questions that can help you close the sale and don't make up any answers just to close the sale.

However, add this statement:

To show my commitment to you, I have decided to give everyone who applies now the discount and all the bonuses.

So if you're experiencing fear of missing out (FOMO), you haven't. Don't feel any time pressure. I'm just going to go ahead and give it to everybody because I'm having a great time. My goal is to help you and if that's what it takes to get you to enrol, so you can get the help that you want and get the results that you're after, then I'm committed to doing exactly that. I want to work with you. So if you have a question right now, go ahead and type it in your chat box. I'm going to start reviewing them right now and I'll answer them live. So here we go.

Then you're set to dive deep into the Q&A session.

What comes next

Overall, these are the nine structures in proper sequential order of an awesome webinar to sell high ticket offer. Now you know them, go ahead to prepare your PowerPoint slide, sign up for a webinar platform and host your webinar to sell your high ticket services.

Be aware that you can actually sell high ticket offers starting from $1,000 to $25,000 using this webinar structure. To recap, the steps are from a webinar to an application and to a phone call where you close the client. It doesn't get much simpler than this.

I know that, at this point, you might be wondering what you are going to say on the phone to the client. This book is limited in scope to a high ticket selling webinar structure, but here are the strategies that I personally use in my own business to close sales on the phone. You will need to use an elicitation technique to gather information from the client before you close.

Eliciting information

According to Sam Parker, author of the *Just Sell* blog, you need to have a repertoire of open-ended questions, where the answers given will not be 'yes' or 'no' but the prospect will be involved in the sales conversation and not require leading, prompting or interrupting.

These questions will help you to gather information, qualify the sales opportunities and establish rapport, trust and credibility. The key takeaway is to ask the questions and let the prospective client give you the answers. This is probably going to be the most valuable asset in your sales arsenal as long as you are a keen listener.

Open-ended questions

Here are the open-ended questions that will get you started. Make a note of the ones which are most relevant to your specific industry or, better still, model new ones using those that are relevant. Come up with your own, memorise them, print them out and pass them to your team.

- What are your expectations/requirements for this product/service?
- How do you see this happening?
- What is it that you'd like to see accomplished?
- With whom have you had success in the past?
- With whom have you had difficulties in the past?
- Can you help me understand that a little better?
- What does that mean?
- How does that process work now?
- What challenges does that process create?
- What challenges has that created in the past?
- What are the best things about that process?

- What other items should we discuss?

Qualifying questions

- What do you see as the next action steps?

  What is your timeline for implementing/purchasing this type of service/product?
  What other data points should we know before moving forward?
  What budget has been established for this?
  What are your thoughts?
  Who else is involved in this decision?
  What could make this no longer a priority?
  What's changed since we last talked?
  What concerns do you have?

Questions to establish rapport ,trust and credibility

- How did you get involved in?...

  What kind of challenges are you facing?
  What's the most important priority to you with this ?Why?
  What other issues are important to you?
  What would you like to see improved?
  How do you measure that?

Now go sell something!

(remember: no leading ... no prompting ... no interrupting ... really).

Conclusion

In conclusion, you now have the strategies to sell high ticket services using a webinar. This same exact strategy has proven to work over and over again if only you act on it strongly and decisively. After presenting your webinar live several times, you will be able to gauge the response to track a few things such as the points at which people dropped off or got excited and the number of people who stayed to the end. Keep tweaking your webinar, based on this report, until you have addressed all possible objections, then can you automate it. Better still, you can automate it out of the gate, track and iterate as you go along.

My job is pretty much done at this point and the ball is now in your court. Go ahead to take massive action.

"80 percent of success is just showing up" —Woody Allen

Showing up means…starting.

RESOURCES

Visit our resource page at https://www.trajectorybook.com/resources to claim the following resources that will help you along the way to create an awesome webinar.

FREE checklist that will help you write your webinar script in 60 minutes or less.

FREE webinar funnel that you can immediately deploy to launch your webinar. We have done all the heavy lifting for you- all that you have to do is to replace video, images, text, branding and you are good to go.

FREE strategy call - you will be able to schedule a Free strategy call from the resource page, so that you can get help from me personally to get started.

Also, you will get access to live webinar and evergreen webinar platforms that I personally use to host my webinars.

In the event that you missed the link to all the resources we have for you, here is the link again —> https://www.trajectorybook.com/resources

References

Russell Brunson. Expert Secrets: The underground playbook for growing your company online.

Sam Parker. Just Sell blog

Frank Kern. Highly Paid Advisor

Blair Warren. One sentence persuasion course

www.ingramcontent.com/pod-product-compliance
Lightning Source LLC
Chambersburg PA
CBHW071110240526
45469CB00006BD/2418